Lessons from Summer Camp

Lessons from Summer Camp

poems

Jim Tilley

RED HEN PRESS | *Pasadena, CA*

Lessons from Summer Camp

Book design and layout by Latina Vidolova

Library of Congress Cataloging-in-Publication Data

Names: Tilley, Jim, author.
Title: Lessons from summer camp / Jim Tilley.
Description: First edition. | Pasadena, CA : Red Hen Press, [2016]
Identifiers: LCCN 2015046505 | ISBN 9781597093842 (casebound) | ISBN 9781597093040 (softcover)
Subjects: | BISAC: POETRY / American / General.
Classification: LCC PS3620.I515 A6 2016 | DDC 811/.6—dc23
LC record available at http://lccn.loc.gov/2015046505

The National Endowment for the Arts, the Los Angeles County Arts Commission, the Los Angeles Department of Cultural Affairs, the Dwight Stuart Youth Fund, the Pasadena Arts & Culture Commission and the City of Pasadena Cultural Affairs Division, the Ahmanson Foundation, and Sony Pictures Entertainment partially support Red Hen Press.

First Edition
Published by Red Hen Press
www.redhen.org

Acknowledgments

As always, I would like to thank my wife and agent, Deborah Schneider, for her patient support and critical reading of my work. A special mention goes to my mother, Betty Tilley, who understood from my first day at summer camp what it meant to me. I would like to make amends for the error in my previous collections of neglecting to thank Kate Gale and Mark Cull, co-founders of Red Hen Press, for their unwavering support of my writing. To my fellow poets, Will Wells, Marty Steyer, Charlie Coté, Jim Scruton, and the various members of the Katonah Poetry Series' writing group, I express my gratitude for their critique and suggestions, most of which I took to heart and incorporated into the final version of this collection.

I had the pleasure of revisiting my old summer haunt, Camp Nominingue, in July 2013. The camp director, Grant McKenna, and I chatted about "old times." He had pulled up several documents from my days at the camp and suggested that I might consider writing an article for the camp's monthly newsletter, *Tumpline*. This collection resulted from that suggestion. Grant has graciously published some of the poems in the newsletter.

A final thank you to the founder of the camp, F. M. Van Wagner, who passed away in 1989 at the age of 95, an avid canoe tripper until near the end. "Van," as we used to call the camp's Big Chief, had the foresight in 1925 to realize that a venue among white birches on the shores of Petit Lac Nominingue in the Laurentian Mountains of Quebec would be perfect as a summer camp for boys and that the camp experience would shape those boys for the rest of their lives. He was right.

for all Campers and Counselors at Camp Nominingue,

those who were, still are, or will be

Contents

Rise free from care before the dawn and seek adventures.
Let the noon find thee by other lakes,
and the night overtake thee everywhere at home.

—Henry David Thoreau, "Walden"

It's when I'm weary of considerations,
And life is too much like a pathless wood
Where your face burns and tickles with the cobwebs
Broken across it, and one eye is weeping
From a twig's having lashed across it open.
I'd like to get away from earth awhile
And then come back to it and begin over.

—Robert Frost, "Birches"

New Season

Like a horde of young wizards headed to Hogwarts
(those stories still decades from being written),
we gathered on the platform at Montreal's Windsor Station
in late June, fathers pushing our trunks on trolleys,
mothers fighting back their usual tears, to board the train
for the four-hour voyage into the Laurentian Mountains
and our summer-long stay at camp. The "new boys"
were hesitant, bewildered; the "old boys," together again
after a year apart, smacked each other on the back,
more joyous than they would be at any school reunion.
We were looking forward, not back, the end of summer
infinitely far off. There was little catching up—
talk of school tacitly off-limits—banter about canoe trips
instead, and though we'd never admit it, we, the old boys,
some of us anyway, had become drunk on the camp motto,
not realizing then, not having been told (it would've been
too much like school), that those words we chanted
around the ceremonial fire at Council Ring had been lifted
straight from Thoreau: *Rise free from care before the dawn
and seek adventure. Let the noon find thee by other lakes,
and the night overtake thee everywhere at home.* Some of us
had been homesick all year.

New Boys

Blankets draped over arms, blind-folded
with bandannas, the new boys queued up behind
the Dining Hall at the start of the path
to the Council Ring, youngest in front, oldest
at the rear. Each held the hand of the boy
ahead of him, the first the hand of a Counselor.
Counselors distributed themselves along the line
to keep boys from straying off the path
or stumbling over an exposed root. When the
Big Chief, the Counselors without new boys
in their charge, and the old boys had been seated,
the new boys were led into the Council Ring,
guided to the first tier of bench seats
around the fire pit. All in place, still standing,
they were allowed to remove their blindfolds.
Tent by tent, Counselors presented the new Braves
to the Big Chief and asked that they be accepted
into the tribe. Once admitted, the new boys,
no longer new, wrapped their blankets
around their shoulders, took their seats,
never again having to be initiated—"not quite never"
they'd learn when they became college freshmen,

were hazed by fraternities, admitted into
exclusive clubs. They'd start their first jobs,
later change allegiances, start again.
Would learn that initiation to a strange place
always brings a little fear, like being blind at first,
not knowing quite where you're going, or why.

Feathers

Every new Camper was given a shield he'd bring back
every summer to hang on a wall of the Main Lodge—
a form of report card to record progress in the various
skills taught at camp. A chevron-shaped plaque
made of ash (perhaps it was maple) with smooth, beveled
edge and darker veneer surface on which, over a red
felt mat, was mounted the brass head of an Indian
in elaborate headdress. An achievement was recorded
for all to witness by a long, brass feather inserted
into the headdress, each labeled with the skill—
Archery, Canoeing, Nature Study, Swimming, etc.—
and the level attained—B for beginners, or 1st, 2nd, or 3rd,
the third the ultimate goal. It took a great effort
over many years to fill out the headdress, to replace
firsts with seconds, seconds with thirds, each of us trying
to better the mark set by the legendary Harry Black,
who earned a cumulative fifty-two points.

As a last-year

Senior, I eventually broke blond-haired Harry's record,
my full headdress displaying twenty feathers,
one for every skill, all thirds but four—a second
in rowing (the highest), second in riflery, firsts in boxing

and diving. I still cannot steady my breathing
or trembling hands when aiming a .22 caliber rifle.
Still would rather take flight than fight. I have never
been able to stand on the high board and plunge.

Driftwood

Bored with making paddles and oars, with restoring
totem poles, I asked the head of the woodworking shop
whether fashioning a lamp from a piece of driftwood
would qualify me for my 3rd feather in Woodcraft.
He took me to a pile of stumps and roots, mostly cedar,
behind the shop. Rejecting them all, I said I'd find my own
and walked out to the Senior Swim Area, around the point
to Bullfrog Bay where the low-lying bushes grew right
to the water's edge. Wading through the reeds, picking up
leeches on my legs, brushing away branches that scratched
my thighs, I found a piece that clearly would not work
as a lamp, but was already, even in raw form, a piece of art.
It could have been left as is, but that wouldn't have merited
a 3rd feather, so I took it back to show the head of the shop.
"As with people," he said, "you don't know what you'll find
until you peel away the surface. What grain and color
lies there? What knots and imperfections should you leave
in their natural state? No, there's no lamp here, but give it
a try." My find looked like a man and woman locked in
a dance, the woman bent backward from her waist,
the taller man leaning over her, her arms reaching around
his torso, the couple joined at a common groin that grew

from the piece's base. "Be careful not to carve too deep.
It's easy to cut through the best color, and once you cut,
it won't come back." With the triangular blade of a whittling
knife, I worried the oranges and reds. He showed me how
to make colors richer by rubbing in wax, massaging in
a layer, adding another. "It should last a lifetime," he said.
I gave it to my mother, who displayed it in her living room
until she moved into an old-age home. Now it's back
in my hands, relic sitting on a dresser in the attic.

Metal Tray

We made useful, if inelegant, things for our
mothers, like trays to serve guests
finger sandwiches or biscuits to accompany
afternoon tea. Metal, because that's what
we were given to work with and 3rd feathers
in Metalcraft is what we needed to earn.
But our motives were pure—we made the trays
for our mothers. We worked the unfamiliar
tools bearing names we've long forgotten,
contraptions to secure and shear and shape
the soon-to-be trays. We forced the metal
to yield to our will, painstakingly forming
curls inside curls at the ends. Metal with a
pre-stamped pattern like stitches on a quilt,
sheets of aluminum we fashioned into articles
too small to be truly useful, stenciled
with the camp crest, just an emblem then,
not seen as a symbol of the privilege of being
sent away for a summer.

Lost and Found

For good reason the camp made mothers sew
nametags inside their sons' clothing, including socks
and underwear. No need to tell any mother why,
no reason for most Campers to wince at the weekly
lost and found call-out. Directors would hold up
a piece of clothing in the Dining Hall for everyone
to see, then announce the name. How embarrassing
for a boy to keep traipsing up front to claim
his lost apparel, the stack grown high for the serious
offender, the snickers audible. Occasionally,
to make a point, much as they'd do in their positions
at private school, the Directors would hold a boy
for questioning, ask whether he'd ever stopped
to wonder why he had so little to wear. The rest of us
knew these boys would never be named Leaders
if they lasted long enough to become Seniors.
We knew why their parents sent them away.
Still, the camp was too forgiving—no lesson learned
when the lost is always found and then returned,
embarrassment the only consequence of carelessness.

Nature Study

Devil's Paintbrush, pretty orange wildflower
with a yellow center, fiery colors that belie
the softness of the petals, fine brushlike hairs
used by the Devil Himself, seated at a canvas,
to paint Hell. To some "city boys," who spent
their non-summer lives among cement, brick,
steel, tar, and glass, Nature Study was pure hell.
No need for them to learn that white pines
have bundles of five needles and red pines two,
no need to run a hand across smooth or rough
bark to tell what type of tree, or to examine
the shape of a frond to recognize the genus of fern.
For them and many others, the Nature Cabin
was not a favorite place, not even with its
special attractions: de-scented, black-and-white-
striped skunk penned out front and stuffed
loon with all-black head and black-and-white-
spotted back, suspended in full wingspan from
the ceiling inside. But for me, the Nature Cabin
was more than a place to learn the facts of plant
and animal life. Many days, an hour before
the noon gong, armed with my Brownie camera

and a roll of film, I would lie in wait to capture
the Program Director's daughter as she passed by
in short shorts, tank top, and sneakers without
socks, her blond hair in bangs, on her way
to the Dining Hall to fetch her family's lunch.

Snake and Frog

We'd congregated on the beach, none of us
willing to intervene, too intrigued
to see how Nature's predator and prey
would work things out. Most of us
rooted for the frog as it was slowly ingested—
so slowly it seemed as if the snake
doubted itself, that maybe it had realized
its eyes were bigger than its stomach,
better to disgorge the creature before it
became a fat knot stuck in the throat.
Some of us lost interest and continued towards
the Senior Swim Area, content to let our
more bloodthirsty friends reveal the outcome
later, but others remained, a few ophiophilists
(snake-lovers) changing their allegiance
as less and less of the frog showed.
All the while, the frog remained cool, didn't
struggle to escape, exhibited no signs of distress
as the snake "sucked in" one leg and then
the other, working its way bit by bit
up the abdomen until only the frog's head
protruded from the snake's maw. And then—

the reason that one should always stay
to the end—without any warning, when the
snake must have sensed the game was over,
that it had won the contest of wills and was
perhaps a little greedy for results, the snake
opened its jaws wide, and the frog, as if it knew
its time would come, leapt free and kept
leaping, clever enough to stop only when
safely aboard a lily pad in the bay, where there
was time enough to assess the damage,
but not digest the lesson it had just learned.

Outdoor Chapel

Although the Chapel looked out on Bullfrog Bay,
none of the bullfrogs, which so maddened us at night,
dared disturb the peace on Sunday morning.
As if they knew their time and place or were silenced
by a higher power. The sacred spot in the woods
was mostly shaded, usually a few rays of sunlight
filtering through spruce and birch. (Birches that,
with their hanging peels of paper-thin bark,
might have served as parchment for recording
our solemn thoughts had we not been taught
that stripping off bark would kill the trees.) Our pews
were tiers of railroad ties set into the steep slope
rising from the reeds and lily pads of the bay toward
the Council Ring on the crest of the hill. A small,
two-manual pump organ sat at the front on a platform
next to a short totem pole, more dais than altar.
Every Sunday, a Senior Staff member stood behind it,
delivered a brief talk about the spirituality
to be found in Nature and in the experience
of making new friends at summer camp. Attendance
was required, but the service was non-denominational.
Roman Catholics could opt out by taking Mass

at the local Cathedral. In Chapel, Protestants and Jews
sat together. There were no readings from a holy book,
no mention of Jesus, no New Testament stories,
just a few songs and hymns celebrating the outdoors—
All things bright and beautiful, All creatures great and small,
All things wise and wonderful, The Lord God made them all.
No one objected to the presence of God.

Upright Piano

When the powers-that-be discovered I had played
as a substitute organist (though not a good one)
in church, they gave me a key to the pump organ
in the Outdoor Chapel. That was fine, but I could play
the old upright piano on the veranda of the Senior Lodge
whenever I wanted since it was never locked. Although
anyone was permitted to play it, few did, most Campers
probably forced to take lessons during the school year
and happy to escape for the summer. Exposed to the
elements, the piano had aged well beyond its years.
The soundboard was warped and the ivories had yellowed,
chipped, and split. The piano was tuned only once a year.
For a rank amateur like me, there was something
comforting about a piano badly out of tune, as if one's
mistakes weren't mistakes at all, but intentional variations
on the original piece. No true musician would buy that;
no true musician would play such a piano, but there
were few true musicians at camp, because such people
were different from us and were sent to a different
camp. To the uninitiated, it must have sounded as if I knew
what I was doing—my playing was good enough to earn
a 3rd in Entertainment by performing before the assembled

Campers and Counselors in The Theatre one evening.
I was fortunate that it was a mandatory event, for who
would want to hear me play and then watch a skit written,
acted, and directed by *Campers?* I played Rachmaninoff's
"Prelude in C# Minor," which I'd performed a few months
earlier at my music teacher's June recital. Though the score
called for my favorite chords to be rendered *pianissimo,*
I pounded them *pesante* and *fortissimo* with silent regrets
to the composer turning in his grave. I didn't like performing
in public, but I needed my 3rd feather. So I imagined I was
still on the veranda, at peace among the birches, free
to try any piece, no matter how difficult. I returned home
a somewhat practiced pianist, much to the wonderment
of my piano teacher, who'd expected me to slack off
all summer, as I had during the year. If she were alive now,
she'd be surprised to hear that I still play, not often
and not well, except for the Rachmaninoff.

Bullfrog Bay

We were fifteen, Seniors. On the nights that refused
to cool off, the bullfrogs croaked back and forth
to one another in Bullfrog Bay, building to a crescendo
directed against us, a dissonant orchestra shaking
our eardrums, the booming beats drowning out
all other sound, even the crickets' violins.
It started as a joke on one such night, one person's idea,
passed from tent to tent as we suffered the cacophony—
the thought that we could silence them with a thwack
from the flat side of a paddle, knock them off their
lily pads one by one. Under a full moon in a clear sky,
we mounted a posse, two to a canoe, and began
the hunt, our shouts louder than the croaks
we'd set out to extinguish, battle cries rising to a pitch
that drove the work of slaughter. It lasted an hour.

Campcraft

The camp set aside an area for teaching proper use
of machete, axe, and knife—blazing and clearing trails,
chopping down trees, splitting logs, shaving kindling
for fires. How to pitch a tent, make a mattress
from balsam, erect a lean-to with a canoe and tarp.
Repair tears in the canvas along the bottom of a canoe
with a candle and stick of "canoe glue." It took years
of improving those skills for a Camper to earn a 3rd
feather in Campcraft. Surprising that so few have
proved useful. No one ever won over a woman by
building her a lean-to. If the space between spouses
turns into wilderness, no axe or machete is going
to cut a path through it. None of us have applied
canoe glue to the tears in life. None of us thought about
those things as adolescents.

Council Ring Fire

Once a week we'd sit in the stands at Council Ring
and wait for a Camper to initiate the evening's challenges.
"O Big Chief, I, Brave Pyromaniac from the Wigwam
Kiamika, would like to challenge three other Braves
to a string-burning contest." And from various parts
of the stands, three boys (pre-picked to prevent
embarrassment to the challenger), one after another
in rapid-fire echo, "O Big Chief, I accept this challenge."
Then each Brave, given his own pre-split cedar log,
would whittle shavings as fast as he could to stack
beneath a string strung two feet above the ground.
Invariably, one of the challengers, braver than the rest,
would light his pile of curled shavings quickly in a gamble
while continuing to slice long thin spikes to plant amidst
his dying blaze. The trick was to coax flames
to reach high enough at their peak to lick at the string
and burn it through. The victor, the risk-taker perhaps,
years later a senior executive of an upstart company,
might set the world on fire, outperform his competitors,
become the next Big Chief, take his rightful place
at the head of the Council Ring, flanked by colored totems
on the boardroom walls. Or maybe a lesser Brave

would wear the brass ring, a boy who'd regularly failed
the weekly challenges yet found his stride later in life,
someone who never got to say, "O Big Chief, I humbly accept
the role of Firemaker tonight, and light the ceremonial fire."

Indians & Settlers

As young children, we played Cowboys & Indians
after school. With six-shooters and bows we killed each other,
but all the dead would resurrect to fight again.
There was no immortality granted in Indians & Settlers,
the variation we played at camp. There, when you were dead,
you were really dead, sent back from the woods
to sit out the rest of the game. No do-overs.
No rubber-tipped arrows or imaginary bullets in that game,
just bandannas. You'd tuck yours into the back of your pants,
leaving one-half exposed. Indians wore red, Settlers white.
Both Red and White would hide their team's flag
in a small clearing in the woods so it could easily be seen.
Your team tried to find and capture the other's flag first,
carry it back to Indians & Settlers Field, and plant it
between your goalposts. Your personal goal was to stay alive
to help your team, not let the enemy snatch your bandanna
before you could snatch his. Boy-to-boy, it was a test
of strength and quickness. Team-to-team, more a question
of strategy. Who would scout, who attack, who defend?
Should you travel alone or in packs? Defend close to your flag
or back at the field? The game sorted out leaders
from followers, the brave from the lily-livered.

In my first game, I died early in a skirmish, thrown down
by a larger boy, flipped over, and quickly relieved
of my bandanna. I sat out most of the game. After that,
regardless of the role I was assigned by our team's captain,
I would find a good hiding place and lie in wait.
Ambush only the boys I knew I could beat. Attack a lone boy,
never a pack. Some called that cowardly, and I suppose
it was. I knew I was less valuable to my team
than the quickest and strongest, but no value at all if dead.
And though I learned to hide from others in those woods,
I knew it for what it was. Hadn't yet rationalized it as
merely knowing one's place in battle. Didn't understand
that not all battles are the same.

J-Stroke and Sweep

You can't see the metaphor when you're a Camper
or Counselor. You're not looking for it.
A canoe is just a canoe, a paddle just a paddle.
At camp, you learn the J-stroke to keep your canoe
on course. You practice it, intrigued that a straight
stroke modified at its end with a flourish, the lower
hand on the paddle turning out and away from the canoe
to form a letter J (or its mirror image), allows you
to maintain course. Later in life, you see people
out on rivers and lakes who think that paddling
first on one side, then the other, back and forth,
is the proper way to keep a canoe headed straight.
Sometimes you see them sitting in the stern,
their weight too far back, the bow out of the water.
Better to sit in the bow seat facing backwards,
you'd like to tell them. You know. But the canoe is
wider there, and they'd have to shift from side to side
to paddle alternately on the left and right. At camp,
you learned to kneel in the center, straddling
the portage thwart, one leg over it and one up against it
from behind, as if you were praying to the god of wind.
And if that god's wind is heavier than a breeze, and if

you're traveling broadside to the waves—because that is your intended course—you soon learn it's a different stroke you require. You must paddle on the leeward side with a broad, sweeping motion that pushes the bow back into the wind. At camp, the J-stroke and sweep work well. It's only later you discover their limitations. As a Counselor, you had experience with children, other people's, not yours—you had them in your care only for the summer. Less commitment, the stakes not as high. But with your own, there's seldom anything as simple as J-stroke and sweep to keep matters in balance. And in marriage, too, the winds shift constantly. No technique or tool or amount of practice seems adequate, and often it's not as much a question of staying the course as finding where you need to go.

War Canoes

They were used by returning "two-nighters"
for the final leg of their canoe trips,
the paddle across the home lake back to camp.
The long, wide canvas canoes painted a hunter green
could accommodate fifteen. They also figured
in the camp's Tribal Games, all Campers
and Counselors assigned to one of six tribes
for a weekend of competition, everybody's face
painted and repainted in war stripes
throughout the Games—
Huron yellow, Sioux green, Algonquin red,
Blackfoot black, Cree blue, or Iroquois orange.
Contests of campcraft and athletic skill,
ultimately settled on water in a series of canoe races,
culminating in the grand finale—
tribes squaring off in the war canoes,
two at a time in a quarter-mile sprint. Two legs,
one out and one back, with a big turn around a mark
that invariably won or lost the race,
the boys on one side of the canoe making broad
sweeping strokes with their paddles,
the boys on the other in simultaneous reverse sweep,

the Counselor in the stern leaning hard
on his paddle to lever the turn,
the bowman-turned-coxswain shouting,
"Stroke . . . Stroke . . . ," holding his paddle firmly
against the gunwale to form a bow rudder
that sharpened the turn. Each pair of tribes faced off.
At the end, the top two raced against each other,
the outcome often determining the overall victor
in the Games. The less powerful team
sometimes won that final race, having by then
finely honed their technique, all working as one
to pivot the canoe about its center and build a cushion—
precious seconds no brawn could overcome.

Portage

Before departing camp for the wild, a Counselor
prepares his canoe for portaging
with rope, two paddles, and a tump strap.
He uses the rope to rig the portage thwart,
and attach the tump strap at each end to the gunwales
just forward of the thwart. He inserts
the blades of the paddles into the rigging,
ties the shafts to the sides of the bow seat.
With knees bent, he stands at the middle of the canoe,
grasps it with both hands at the near gunwale,
lifts it to rest on his thighs. Leaving his right hand
on the near gunwale, he reaches over with his left,
grasps the far gunwale. He rocks the canoe
gently on his thighs, takes a deep breath.
In a single, smooth motion rolls it upside down
while raising it clear over his head
with both arms extended. Then lowers it slowly,
exhales, letting his head pass through the gap
between the paddles so that their blades
rest on his shoulders. He places the tump strap
between the blades and across the top of his head
and adjusts the tumpline until the canoe

lies barely above his shoulders with the tump taut.
At the start of the trip's first portage, he will check
his preparation by standing for a minute,
arms hanging loosely at his sides, the inverted canoe
perfectly balanced on his head, its full weight
distributed down his spine and throughout his body.
Then he'll depart from the lakeside put-in,
start along the trail, man and canoe as one.

Echo Island

It was the preferred destination to take the younger boys on their first canoe trip. Three days, two nights away from the comfort of their beds on the platform tents at camp. I can't remember whether it was the big or little kidney-shaped lake that the island inhabited, Lac Rognon or the Petit version, a small dot of land rising high above the water, sprinkled with white pine and red maple, areas of smooth, exposed rock from which it was safe to dive. Plenty of open space on the crest to pitch a tent for five Campers, the two Counselors bedding down a hundred feet away under their overturned canoes raised at one end and draped with a tarp. For mattresses, boughs of balsam cut onshore and ferried to the island along with a day's supply of wood. Down closer to the water, a fire pit over which we made oatmeal and bacon for breakfast, chicken noodle soup and grilled tuna fish sandwiches for lunch, creamed corn and boiled potatoes to accompany canned corned beef for dinner. In the evening, we'd sit around the fire—all seven—our patter dying down as night squeezed the last light from the day. Lying on our backs, we'd wait for the Milky Way to appear. If we were lucky, we'd hear the call of a loon, soon followed by its repeat

from the surrounding hills. Sometimes two loons would
echo each other's calls, as if one were lost and the other
were saying "I'm over here." If you woke in a mist
that had fallen during the night and found you couldn't
see as far as shore, you'd shout "Echo ... Echo ... "
and wait for the hills to return a message, "Rest assured—
we are here and your way back is out there . . . somewhere."

Night Overtake Thee

Everywhere is home—something you might hear
a Buddhist say. At peace with the world
around you, easier, you've found, on a canoe trip
than back home. You pass through lakes
and pause, as water drips from the end
of your paddle resting across the gunwales,
to take in what you can't see but only feel.
If noon finds you by other lakes,
so will night, a new place or an old one
revisited. You cook a meal over an open fire,
eat a wild-blueberry pie you baked in
a reflector oven, its crust rolled thin on the hull
of your canoe with a tin can. You launch
a lifetime love of cooking. You pitch your tent
under pines, listen to them talk in the wind.
They try to tell you something
you won't hear until many years later.
Most nights you find clarity in the darkness
of the wilderness, let your mind run free.
More stars than you ever expected to see.
Up there, alien places where you can imagine
beings by other lakes, loons calling to them too.

Tonight, you find yourself at home in the forest
of another galaxy. Tomorrow, morning mist
will rise and you'll watch a doe drink cautiously
on the far side, sensing she is not alone.
You'll discover a lake that is clear to the bottom,
fill your pannikin to quench your thirst.

Water Wheel

You'd line up for the main attraction
in the Junior Swim Area, chest deep
in water. When it was your turn,
you'd climb the ladder on the side,
step onto the top of the wheel
where you'd try to maintain balance
as long as possible by peddling
backwards or forwards at a pace
fast enough to keep the wheel turning,
slow enough not to get flung off,
all the while ignoring the heckling
of those waiting for your inevitable
fall. Nothing you could do about it,
a matter of some physical force
waiting to pounce on you the moment
you faltered. You didn't realize
there were several factors, not all
physical, that could quickly put you
off your game, send you spinning
out of control to land on your ass
or take a nosedive. But because you
were only a child back then, it was

always water you landed in, the fall
broken softly with a splash. When you
surfaced, you'd swim to the back
of the line, thinking that if you merely
kept trying, you'd conquer this game.

Swimming Lessons

Many of us already knew how to swim well by the time
we first arrived at camp, having been taught
by our mothers or fathers during picnics at lakes.
We knew how to swim freestyle or "crawl" as it was
called back then. Or thought we did. We knew
we hadn't yet grasped the proper technique
for other strokes. Sidestroke was so easy it hardly
needed to be taught, but breaststroke and backstroke—
they were harder. The head swimming instructor,
Mr. Titus, was relentlessly demanding—he'd stand
atop the tower at the Senior Swim Area to take
a bird's-eye view of our every flaw, the left leg
in the "whip kick" not sweeping its arc symmetrically
with the right, a foot flexed when it should be
pointed, the head submerged too far in this stroke
or that, the kick always too vigorous, fingers splayed
wide apart when they should have been held together
loosely. "You don't have webbed hands," he'd say.
His surname spoke to a certain Romanesque strength,
and watching him pull himself through the water
seemingly with arms alone, only the upper half
of his body visible, an occasional flutter from his feet

piercing the surface, we couldn't help but wonder if he
were merely half a man, nothing below the waist.
Breathing alternately to the left and right, his mouth
opened into a perfect letter O, each exhale a barely
audible cleansing breath, he propelled his torso
with slow, steady strokes, lap after lap for an hour.
Mesmerizing, monotonous. When he finally emerged
from the water, utterly relaxed as if he'd just stepped
out of a steaming shower, we were sure he wasn't
entirely human. We knew we could never be like him.
Still, when we became Counselors, he trusted us
to teach the young boys, supporting them under their
backs or stomachs to let them get the sense of floating,
then kneeling beside them in shallow water, our faces
submerged, showing them how to breathe more and more
slowly, until it seemed they were hardly breathing at all.

Lifesaving Lessons

We practiced in pairs, one locking the other
in a death-grip. We'd learned how to break
strangleholds; we'd rehearsed the moves
again and again on the beach, out of water,
in air we could breathe easily while attempting
to escape. Only when we knew them cold,
when they'd truly become second nature,
did the instructors let us try them in water
over our heads, where, locked together
as we sank, it was impossible to breathe.
After hundreds of attempts, we learned to relax,
not panic. Learned not to leap in and engage
a struggling swimmer, except as a last resort.
Throw a lifeline first. Extend an oar or pole.
But it wasn't until a few years after leaving camp
for good, one weekend while out picnicking
with friends, that I needed to apply those skills.
Swimming away from the raft on which I
was sunbathing, a young man cramped up
and cried for help. There was no lifeguard
present. No boat nearby. Nothing with which
I could reach out to him—so I jumped in,

forgetting how quickly a drowning person can
clutch you around your neck and take both of you
down. I'd never experienced how strong
someone fearing for his life can be. Unable to
break his grip, I gave him a shot in the groin
that made him go limp. Then cupping his chin,
I hauled him to the raft, life-saving-style, exactly
as we'd been taught at camp. And suddenly
remembering how vital it is to assert control,
I told him to relax, everything would be fine,
and that if he tried to grab me again, I'd have to
kick his fucking brains in. Assured him I would.

Lake Swim

Not a requirement for a 3rd in Swimming,
just a test of endurance, I kept telling myself
about the Lake Swim. Little longer than
half a mile. A goal only for the "best" swimmers,
those who'd swum for their school teams,
competed in national championships.
Trivial for them, merely a practice session,
warm-up for a much longer distance,
not a true test of their skill. Leave it to them.
Let them brag about doing the crawl
all the way across the lake instead of the lowly
sidestroke I knew I'd have to resort to.
But even the best were required to have a cord
cinched around their waist, long tether
to the accompanying rowboat, umbilicus
to the mothership. Unable to shake the feeling
of having to swim endlessly in an infinite sea,
I could never overcome the fear. Yet I could
tread water for an hour. So I kept telling myself
I would try, do it before my time ran out,
but I just kept treading water, not ever letting
them tie that rope around my waist.

Running Free

Campers would rather trim sails than hear about
close hauled and broad reach,
clew and luff, halyards and sheets,
the rules of racing and right-of-way.
Bow and stern, port and starboard, they could abide,
but they wanted to get their hands on a rope,
their feet under hiking straps. Wanted to
sail in a stiff breeze so the boat could heel.
Couldn't wait for the day when they graduated
to skip and took the tiller. All were eager to race
before they'd learned to bring the boat safely
into dock and secure it in a finger, yet too few
learned that winning a race often means
sailing well on the upwind leg where the boats
are at their slowest and it's all about being the best
close hauled—that was "boring," they said;
they wanted to run free.

Tetherball

One summer, late in my life as a Camper, we arrived at camp
to find metal poles installed among the Junior,
Intermediate, and Senior tents (shorter for the younger boys,
whose reach seldom extended as far as they hoped),
a volleyball-like ball attached to the top of each pole
by a length of nylon rope. I'd never played tetherball before,
never even heard of the game, assumed
the camp's powers-that-be must have decided that boys
needed more one-on-one to develop into men.
I came to see the game as a good way to work out
disagreements, one Camper against the other on opposite sides
of an argument, one batting the ball clockwise,
the other counterclockwise, the goal to wrap the rope
all the way around in your direction, the full length of it
spiraling like stripes on a barbershop pole.
The taller and stronger had an advantage—don't they always?—
but occasionally one of us not so blessed would stumble
onto a strategy that briefly negated their edge.
We might catch an opponent's strike
earlier than he expected and send the ball back his way
before he was prepared to swipe at it. Sometimes he'd miss
the ball entirely and you could get a second whack

before he recovered, sometimes even a third or fourth
if he were totally discombobulated, more and more of the rope
wrapping around the pole, the free length getting
shorter and shorter and higher and higher
as an adversary lost his sense of timing. Most often
the stronger boy won, but not always. The strangest thing
was that after a hard-fought match, it was difficult to remember
what had brought the two of you to square off
in the first place, all that piss and vinegar (no, never venom)
spent on punching the ball instead.

Bull's Eye

Before a pattern of concentric circles came to be
used as a target, archers of old would sharpen
their skills by aiming at a bull's skull, the goal to hit
an eye. Tough on the arrows, their piles crashing
into hard bone. It's hard to imagine enough
bulls to supply targets for all the archers then in
the world, this story perhaps apocryphal.
The camp offered two kinds of targets—small,
black-and-white versions at the rifle range where
we fired .22's and large, colored ones at the archery
range where we used camp-made bows of ash.
Bows & Arrows seemed more sporting. We learned
the parts of the arrow—hen and cock feathers,
notch, shaft, and pile—and learned how high to
aim, how to correct for wind. I liked the whistling
sound an arrow made through the air and the
thwack as it pierced the target and sank deep into
a bale of hay, that sound always more satisfying
when the arrow found gold, the center bull's eye.
We were taught how to withdraw an arrow
from the target, a hand against the bale, forefinger
and middle finger straddling the shaft, using

the other hand to jiggle the arrow, loosen its hold,
tugging until it came free. One year the ante
was upped—new targets with life-size posters
of rabbits, squirrels, and chipmunks—motionless
game becoming the sport, as if it would be a thrill
to gut and skin the kill, cook it up for dinner.
What I remember most about archery is the sting
of the bowstring whipping against the inside
of my left arm, which held the bow, swollen after
an hour aiming for the bull's eye. I refused to quit
until ten arrows in a row had hit the mark.

Long Jump and Discus

Discus never became my event. No matter how much
I trained, learned to pace my body's spin and rise
before uncoiling, even my best throws—
the ones when the discus launched without wobble
and caught the air just right, when the black
plastic disc sailed off like an airplane wing lifting
into the sky—barely made the mark required to earn
a 3rd feather in Athletics. Not so for the long jump.
The summer after my freshman year in high school,
I learned to "run in air." I've never understood why
continuing to stride during the jump adds so much
distance, length that should come from speed
and thrust alone, but doesn't. I jumped twenty feet,
well past the needed mark. During a leap, I was
in the zone, and time would seem to slow, as if I were
walking on air. I have long since stopped competing,
but still live it in my dreams, where time almost stops
and in the slowest of slow motions, I sprint down
the runway, arms slicing through the air. I step
perfectly on the board for takeoff, leap higher than
ever, and never come down to Earth.

Lights Out

It was no challenge back then to quiet my mind
after the palaver in the dark suddenly stilled
to sporadic words, then nothing . . .
Sheer exhaustion was enough, and if not,
the humming of crickets, wind in the leaves,
the splashing of waves . . . Much easier back then
when those were real and close at hand,
harder now when merely remembered,
harder to let go, extinguish the excitements
and disappointments now that I carry mine
and my children's, my wife's . . .
It's always a night in the wilderness, but there's
no popping of a fire's dying embers
to distract me; it's no longer as simple as
killing the last pesky mosquito whining
in my ear. There's no Officer of the Day
to call Lights Out!, nobody but me
to shut down the background chatter in my brain,
lower the wick and snuff out the lantern,
my wife having long since gone to sleep.

Officer of the Day

Sounds as if it might be important, someone
who makes the big decisions, runs the show—
after all, it was a Counselor's job.
Turned out to be a position you didn't want
to be assigned to, timekeeper mostly,
ringer of the great bell outside the Main Lodge
for the key markers of the day: Wake-up Call,
First and Second Morning Instruction,
Morning Swim, All Boats In, Afternoon Program,
Afternoon Swim, All Boats In, Evening Program.
Not the breakfast, lunch, or dinner gong—
that was the province of the kitchen staff
and required a hammer. No bell for Lights Out,
just bellowing through a red megaphone
in the various sections of camp when the boys
had to stop their reading and conversation,
turn in for the night. But the Officer of the Day
did preside in the Dining Hall, got to say grace,
never a moment for improvisation, you soon
learned, nothing above and beyond the mundane
Bless this food to Thy use and us to Thy service,
no explicit mention of deities by name. Let's be

plain—it was a boring job, but someone had to
do it and you were responsible for maintaining
the register of canoes and rowboats signed out
and back in. You tried to put a good face on it,
tell yourself it was an opportunity to lounge
in the sun and read, when you could possibly
manage it in fits and starts with incessant chatter
in the background. You hoped it wouldn't
be raining when it was your turn.
You had to walk the tent line nine times a day
shouting the time signatures of the bells you'd just
rung so long and loud you could hardly hear.
But you got to raise and lower the Canadian flag.

The Tent

Except for Seniors, who lived two or three together
without a Counselor, six boys and a Counselor
occupied a large platform tent, two bunks on each side,
two at the back, one in the center. It was mostly
a place to lie down for a mandatory hour of rest
after lunch, and at night, when, before Lights Out,
the Counselor would read or tell stories
to the Junior boys, let the Intermediates read
to themselves or talk. He'd light the kerosene lantern,
adjust its wick for the most light possible
without a sooty flame, but bright enough only
for him to read. The rest of us used flashlights.
Just like at home under our mothers' scrutiny,
we had to keep our space clean. Once a week for
inspection, we'd straighten everything, gather
the clothes hanging on the side poles and conceal them
in a trunk until the designated Counselor-Inspector
had moved on. One tent in each section was declared
winner, and the same tent always seemed to win,
as if there had been an under-the-table payment
by the resident Counselor. Or maybe it was just that
he and his boys were the most obsessive-compulsive,

sweeping not only the platform, but also the ground
around the tent. They'd roll up the flaps tightly,
shake the canvas fly clear of twigs and leaves and wipe
the lantern's globe spotless—you couldn't find a speck
of dust or dirt anywhere after they'd finished.
You wondered who'd they grow up to be, certainly not
like the rest of us who couldn't understand the point.
It was not as if some power-that-be had decreed
that cleanliness was next to anything important, or next
to anything at all. Not even in and of itself, thank God.

Wash-Up

It started with Clean-Up. Every Friday,
in the time slot for Afternoon Program, all Campers
conscripted to render the camp property pristine.
Organized and paraded around like a chain gang
with invisible chains, we picked up litter
in the woods, on paths, around buildings,
and placed it rain-barrel incinerators to burn,
a process that guaranteed we'd be filthy afterwards.
The rest? . . . It stemmed from a problem of trust,
the powers-that-be fully understanding
that boys will be boys when it comes to hygiene.
So they commandeered Afternoon Swim as well,
all Campers required to congregate
naked on the beach. Lake residents knew
the appointed hour. Always on time, the same few
would appear in their motorboats and set anchor
as if they'd been waiting all week. They had their own
box seats. Some of us wanted to swim out
and capsize those boats, but we weren't even permitted
to shout at the interlopers, the lake being public property.
The more boisterous among us did anyway
and called them "perverts" and "sick."

We lathered up and scrubbed one another's backs—
only the hard-to-reach places; the rest we handled alone.
Once rinsed, we'd queue up dripping wet
in front of one of the Senior Staff-Inspectors,
whom we did not dare call perverts or sick,
who'd lift our arms, inspect our pits and crotches,
hair and necks, peer behind our ears,
to make certain we'd removed the week's grime
from our unclean bodies. They'd check us off "the list,"
knowing the powers-that-be would be satisfied,
on behalf of absent parents, that their boys were spic-
and-span in all the right places. For a day. The voyeurs
lifted anchor and left. Until the following week.

Houses of Parliament

How long they'd been called that, Lower House,
primarily for the Juniors, and Upper House
for the Intermediate and Senior Campers,
we never found out, but long before our time,
the foul smell emanating from them
must have inspired the eminent names.
The Counselors had to use them, too, no place
of greater refinement available to the bosses
of our summer lives. Out beyond the tent line,
out there in the valley on the way back from
the Dining Hall, the Houses were outhouses
in every sense. Quiet places in the woods
for time out from the daily routine—
after breakfast, to contemplate the coming
events; after lunch, an interlude to start
to digest what you'd just taken in and expel
what you'd hadn't yet absorbed; in the evening,
right before bed, as darkness began to
blanket everything except the thin lines
of the birches, a moment to get beyond
the biting of the insistent mosquitoes attracted
by the pervasive stink and pass a new piece

of legislation. Our friends from below the
border didn't mind the imposition of a different
form of democracy, though one day, courtesy
of their overnight efforts, we awakened to new
signs on our places of congress—same two
chambers, same stalls, same wicked stench,
but now marked *House of Representatives*
and *Senate*. All the toilet paper was gone.

Counselors' Cabin

There's something about a club you don't belong to.
A curiosity, perhaps envy. Or worse, if you
don't belong because you can't, the rules
excluding you and your type. You stay away from those
and find the ones who will take you, indeed
welcome you. You don't allow yourself to think about
the people who aren't permitted to join;
you take your membership for granted. But all that
was a lesson for later in life. At summer camp,
the only exclusions were places you couldn't be
because you weren't yet old enough—Juniors
not permitted in the Senior Lodge, Intermediates
and Juniors not allowed to venture into Senior Camp.
Those were special places you could dream about
but had to wait to enter until it was your time.
So it was for all of us Campers, wondering
what went on in the Counselors' Cabin.
We hung around it every day, the canoe and paddle
racks just outside, the Tuck Shop next door.
Could they smoke in there? Play poker?
Have snacks between meals? Drink beer?
Was there a stash of *Playboy* magazines?

It didn't occur to us they merely wanted a place
to get away, that being a Counselor was actually a job
from which you might need a little time off,
that we Campers weren't always easy to tolerate.
Mostly they played bridge I found out when I became
a Junior Counselor at sixteen. No betting,
no calendar girls pinned to the walls, no special
flush toilets, no alcohol—they had rules, too.

Letters

Once a week, during the Rest Hour after lunch,
all Campers were forced to write a letter.
Most any letter was considered good enough,
usually one sent off to parents for the younger boys,
possibly to a girlfriend for the older boys,
and after the first ten days of camp, every Counselor
was required to write a letter to the parents
of each boy under his care in his tent, a note
that invariably glossed over what wasn't working,
and fabricated, as necessary, things that were—
a cheery, upbeat account of the thrills
their son was experiencing for the first time at camp,
or again, as he had last year. Fill in the blanks.
Imagine my parents' surprise when they
compared a letter they'd received from my brother
with the one from his Counselor. Everyone
had thought that my brother, seven years younger,
was destined to have the same gleeful
experience as I had as a Camper. His letter
featured a stick-figure sketch of his Counselor,
which he labeled R.F. How sweet, my parents thought.
The letter was typical of a Camper's note home—

short, conveying little that was illuminating,
apart from, in my brother's situation,
his dislike of the nine-hole golf course with its
too-short holes and its dirt "greens."
R.F.'s letter mentioned that my brother had been
found one night, by a Counselor patrolling
after Lights Out, with his feet protruding from
his sleeping bag. My brother had worked his way in
head-first, his way, we learned later,
of muffling his sobs. Rat Fink had been right—
my brother wasn't having a good time.
They'd assumed he was another me. He wasn't.

Visitors' Day

Picnic Beach raked clean, extra tables scattered about,
Counselors on duty along the road into camp
to direct parents to park in the Campcraft Area—
Visitors' Day, a day I could never figure out
whether parents looked forward to
more than their sons, an opportunity to gauge that all
was well, a gamble of sorts, because if all was not
well, there was little that could be done,
homesick Campers seldom allowed by their parents
to leave prematurely after all those non-refundable fees
had already been paid. How I felt
changed during the course of the day, anticipation
at the start, waiting for my parents' car to crest the hill,
hoping they wouldn't be the last to arrive.
It was a chance to show off what I'd learned
during the first few weeks, and, I suppose, an affirmation
that I was missed. (They always put on a good show.)
One year, my grandparents came along
and brought a picnic. We spent the morning at the beach
and swam under the watchful eye of a lifeguard,
no need to pair up with a buddy that day,
no random whistles to check that everyone was present

and accounted for, a little freedom
from the normal routine. I remember showing my parents
my improved proficiency with an axe,
chopping a poplar log into sections, then splitting those
for firewood, saying I wanted an axe of my own
back home. "But we have no trees," my father said
too quickly. "At least none I want cut down."
By the end of Visitors' Day, I was ready for all guests
to leave, certain that enough politeness had been served up,
the invasion having lasted too long, the call of friends
once again overpowering the call of family.
But when my parents' car disappeared around the bend,
I'd always, even as a Senior Camper, find myself
wiping tears from my cheeks, as I do now
when my grown sons leave after a visit home.

The Theatre

The Theatre didn't exist when I first attended camp,
but it must have replaced another structure
because I remember we called it The *New* Theatre.
I visited camp for a day last summer as an alum.
The New Theatre is now fifty years old,
known simply as The Theatre. Standing in the center
aisle in front of the stage, an old upright piano
off to the left, I recalled playing Rachmaninoff
for my 3rd in Entertainment, not to thunderous applause,
but to polite handclaps that acknowledged,
if not celebrated, the end of my performance.
The allure of The Theatre was not
Campers' Entertainment Night but the showing
of the Sunday afternoon movie, never a first-run,
often one we'd seen. (Boys can always
appreciate a James Bond flick one more time.)
The grand finale of the camp season was the musical
a few days before we returned home,
an all-Counselor-and-Staff production featuring
the Senior Staff (the various Directors) in title roles,
sets and costumes labored over all summer,
the Camp Director himself the very model

of a modern Major-General in *Pirates of Penzance*
or the Assistant Business Manager
singing *Food, glorious food! Hot sausage and mustard*
as Oliver Twist. They were great,
the kind of performances you hoped would never end,
the final chorus still singing in your head
as you sank into your pillow on the second-to-last
night of camp. Before leaving The Theatre
on my reunion visit, I sat on the edge of the stage,
thinking back to being in charge of the lighting
my last year as a Senior, cleaning up
and shutting down the place after everyone had left,
one more full day of camp, one final act—
the Senior Bonfire out on the lake at Picnic Beach
in front of The Theatre, all of us gathered in canoes,
singing the camp song as towering flames
consumed the last of the summer's air.

Leaders and Voyageurs

Miniature brass canoes mounted over red felt
at the top of your chevron shield of feathers,
Leader on the left, Voyageur on the right,
the highest awards the camp gave to recognize
the top boys and the master canoe trippers.
You had to be a Senior Camper to be named
a Leader. During the last week of camp, Seniors
speculated about who would make it, who
would get to walk to the front of the Dining Hall
during the final dinner and receive the award,
stand there before all the Campers and wait
to learn who else would be named to the club.
The greatest honor was to become a Leader
at the end of your first year as a Senior so that
everyone would know you were a top boy
when you came back to camp the following year,
a prefect among the rest. To become a Leader,
it helped to be a favorite with the Directors.
Some boys who should have made it, didn't.
But they could become Voyageurs by acquiring
feathers alone—at least seconds in Nature Study
and Cooking, thirds in Campcraft, Canoeing,

and Tripping. No points for being a good guy.
A shield looked bare without any brass canoes,
lacked balance with only one of the top awards.
Most boys wanted both—they could earn the
Voyageur Award on their own, but for the Leader
Award, they had to hope, seldom letting on how
much they coveted it. But you could tell. Partly
by the feigned nonchalance as they dismissed
the possibility, more by what you witnessed
when you returned to the table holding yours—
the faces of the hopefuls who hadn't been called.

Going Home

The white shirts and slacks and jackets
we'd worn on the train to camp
had been stored in the rafters above the ceiling
of the Dining Hall, the camp's only attic.
It was not air-conditioned.
At camp nothing was, except by natural
breezes. Year after year the humidity
would rust the hangers and stain the shirts.
Year after year our mothers applied
lemon juice to take out the rust.
Packing up, saying goodbyes, stepping off
the train at Windsor Station, the last
few handshakes, best wishes—
the end of camp brought a sadness
not even the talk about next summer
could sweep away. Nor could the greeting
smiles of our parents. Once back home,
I started crossing off days on the calendar.
After my last year as a Senior Camper,
before the start of school, I sent in my
application to become a Junior Counselor.
A few years later, there were no more

days to cross off. Time to get a "real job"
my father said. Nearly fifty years later,
retired after a career filled with real jobs,
I knew immediately when I visited
my old summer haunt that it had provided
the tumpline to carry me through.

Biographical Note

Lessons from Summer Camp is Jim Tilley's third book of poetry. His previous collections are *In Confidence* and *Cruising at Sixty to Seventy*. His short memoir, *The Elegant Solution*, has appeared as a Ploughshares Solo e-book, an audiobook through Audible.com, and in a Ploughshares print anthology. His poetry has appeared in *Virginia Quarterly Review, Southwest Review, Alaska Quarterly Review*, and *Southern Review*, among other journals, and has been featured on Poetry Daily and on the PBS News Hour's art blog. He has won Sycamore Review's Wabash Prize for Poetry, the New England Poetry Club's Firman Houghton Award, and an International Publication Award from Atlanta Review. Four of his poems have been nominated for a Pushcart Prize. Tilley earned a doctorate in Physics from Harvard University and worked in insurance and investment banking before retiring. He resides with his wife, Deborah Schneider, in Bedford Corners, New York.